Sunflower Coaster

vibrant sunflower centered on a hexagon-shaped canvas gives you an eye-catching coaster! Stitch several to add a ur-round touch of summer to your decor, or make some for friends to brighten their day!

Level: Intermediate

e: 5¹/₂"w x 5"h

plies: Worsted weight yarn (refer to color key), Uniek® 5" plastic vas hexagon shape, #16 tapestry needle, cork or felt (optional), clear-drying craft glue (optional).

hes Used: Backstitch, French Knot, Gobelin Stitch, Overcast h, and Tent Stitch.

ructions: Follow chart to stitch Coaster. If backing is desired, cork or felt slightly smaller than Coaster and glue to wrong side oaster.

ign by Ann Townsend.

Coaster

COLOR (NL)	COLOR (NL)
gold (11) - 8 yds	blue (32) - 8 yds
brown (13) - 4 yds	dk blue (48) - 5 yds
green (28) - 4 yards	brown (13) Fr. Knot

Safari Coasters

Take a walk on the wild side with our exotic animal print coasters! This set of fringed creations will protect furniture from perilous scratches and spills.

COLOR (NL)	
⬜	white (41)
⬜	gold (17)
⬛	rust (12)
⬜	tan (39)
⬛	black (00)
◯	gold Fringe (17)
◉	black Fringe (00)

Zebra Coaster (29 x 24 threads)

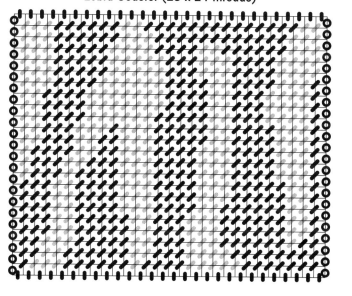

Giraffe Coaster (29 x 24 threads)

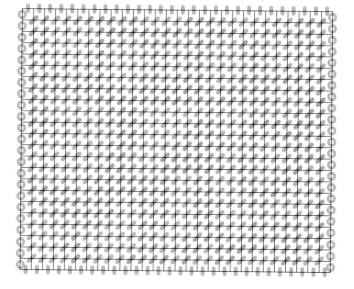

Tiger Coaster (29 x 24 threads)

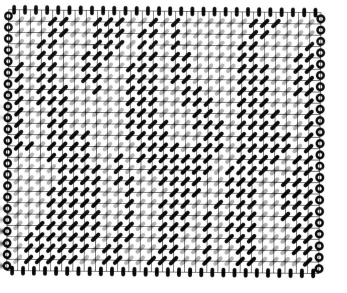

Leopard Coaster (29 x 24 threads)

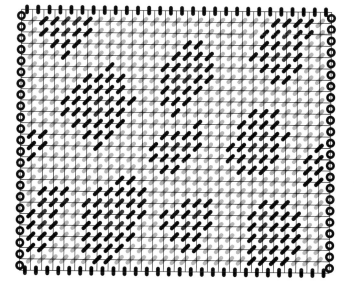

"Sea-sonal" Fun

Coast into summer with this "sea-sonal" coaster! The brightly colored tropical fish makes a perfect poolside or patio accent.

Skill Level: Beginner

Size: 4"w x 4"h

Supplies: Worsted weight yarn (refer to color key), one 10½" x 13½" sheet of 7 mesh plastic canvas, #16 tapestry needle, cork or felt (optional), and craft glue (optional).

Stitches Used: Gobelin Stitch, Overcast Stitch, and Tent Stitch.

Instructions: Follow chart to cut and stitch Coaster. If backing is desired, cut cork or felt slightly smaller than Coaster. Glue cork or felt to back.

Design by Terry A. Ricioli.

Coaster (29 x 29 threads)

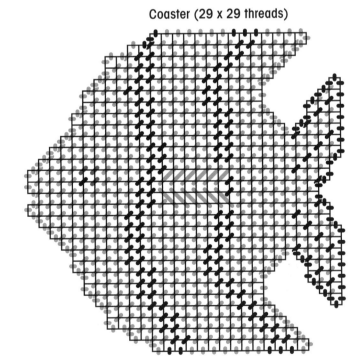

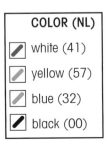

COLOR (NL)	
✎	white (41)
✎	yellow (57)
✎	blue (32)
✎	black (00)

Beautiful Butterflies

1e sound of softly fluttering butterflies is part of nature's symphony. And the winged wonders highlighting these asters are so lifelike that you can almost hear the music. A coordinating storage box completes this collection.

ll Level: Beginner

aster Size: 4⅛"w x 4⅛"h each

der Size: 4⅞"w x 4⅞"h x 1¾"d

pplies: Worsted weight yarn and embroidery floss (refer to color), three 10½" x 13½" sheets of 7 mesh plastic canvas, #16 estry needle, cork or felt (optional), and craft glue (optional).

ches Used: Backstitch, Cross Stitch, French Knot, Gobelin Stitch, ercast Stitch, and Tent Stitch.

Instructions: Use ecru for all joining and to cover unworked edges. Follow charts to cut and stitch Butterfly Coasters Set, completing backgrounds as indicated on charts. Join Top Sides along short edges. Join Top to Top Sides. For Bottom, cut a piece of canvas 30 x 30 threads. Bottom is not worked. Join Bottom Sides along short edges. Join Bottom to Bottom Sides. Cover unworked edges. If backing for Coaster is desired, cut cork or felt slightly smaller than Coaster. Glue cork or felt to back of Coaster.

Designs by Kathleen Hurley.

Continued on page 7.

COLOR (NL)		COLOR (NL)	
⬜	ecru (39)	⬜	dk blue (48)
⬜	lt yellow (20)	⬜	vy lt green (23)
⬜	yellow (57)	⬜	lt green (28)
⬜	vy lt orange (11)	⬜	green (27)
⬜	lt orange (58)	⬜	dk green (29)
⬜	orange (12)	⬜	brown (13)
⬜	dk orange (52)	⬜	dk brown (14)
⬜	lt violet (44)	⬜	vy dk brown (15)
⬜	violet (45)	⬜	black (00)
⬜	dk violet (46)	⬜	*vy dk brown
⬜	vy lt blue (36)	●	*vy dk brown French Knot
⬜	lt blue (35)		*Use 3 strands of embroidery floss.
⬜	blue (32)		

#1 (28 x 28 threads)

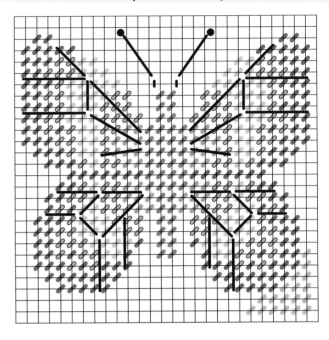

#2 (28 x 28 threads)

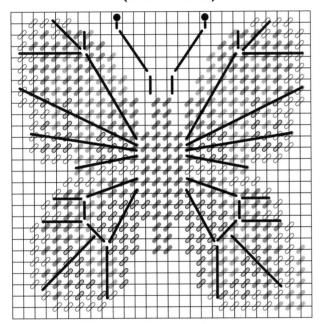

#3 (28 x 28 threads)

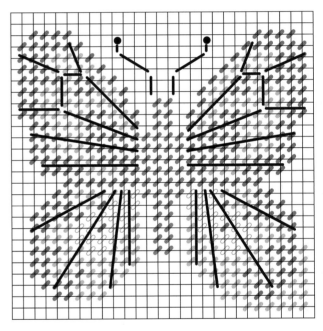

#4 (28 x 28 threads)

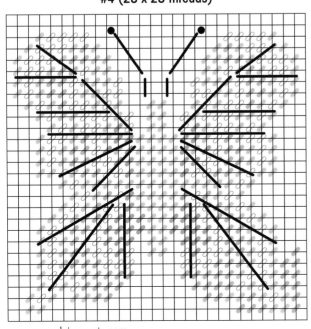

#5 (28 x 28 threads)

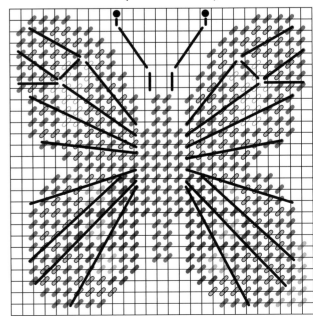

#6 (28 x 28 threads)

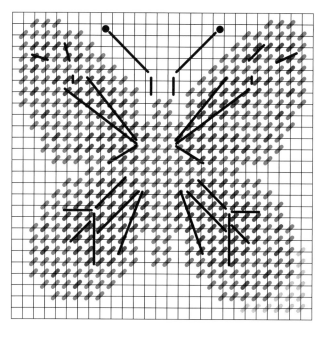

Bottom Side (30 x 16 threads)

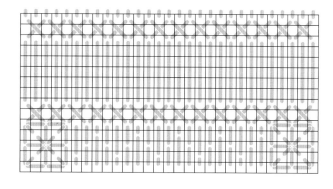

#7 (28 x 28 threads)

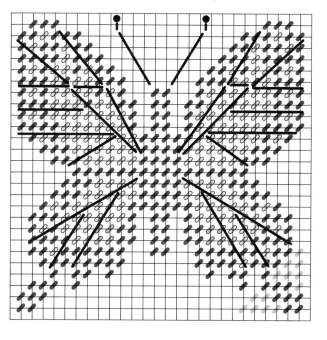

Top Side (32 x 6 threads)

Top (32 x 32 threads)

#8 (28 x 28 threads)

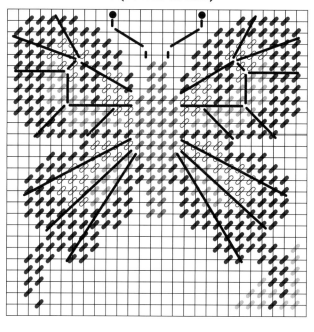

Star-Bright Coasters

itched on star-shaped plastic canvas, our celestial coasters set makes an "out-of-this-world" accent!

ll Level: Intermediate

aster Size: 4³/₄"w x 4³/₄"h each

lder Size: 5¹/₂"w x 5¹/₂"h x 2³/₈"d

pplies: Worsted weight yarn and metallic yarn (refer to color key), e 10¹/₂" x 13¹/₂" sheet of 7 mesh plastic canvas, eight 5" star apes, #16 tapestry needle, 18mm blue bead, sewing needle and ead, 18" of 20 gauge wire, cork or felt (optional), and craft glue ptional).

ches Used: Gobelin Stitch, Overcast Stitch, and Tent Stitch.

tructions: Follow charts to cut and stitch Coaster Set pieces, leaving ches in pink shaded areas unworked. Use metallic copper to cover worked edges of Coasters. If backing is desired, cut cork or felt ghtly smaller than Coaster. Glue cork or felt to back of Coaster. ng metallic copper, join bottom edges of Bottom Side pieces to naining unworked star shape. Referring to photo, use matching or yarn to join Bottom Sides along long edges. Bend wire to nform to unworked edges of Bottom Sides. Using blue overcast ches, cover unworked edges of Bottom Sides and wire. Using blue ercast stitches, join Top Sides along short edges. Working stitches pink shaded area, join Top Sides to Top. Referring to photo, tack d to Top.

sign by Kathy Wirth.

Coaster (stitch 6)

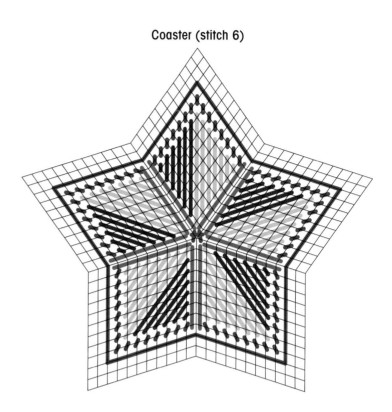

Top

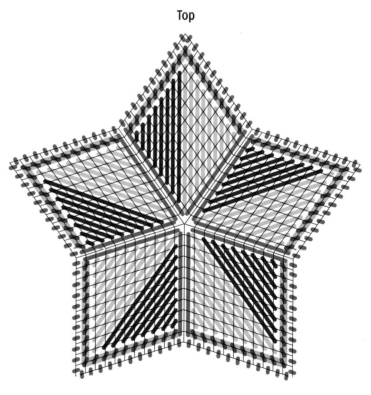

COLOR (NL)	
yellow (57) - 25 yds	
blue (32) - 50 yds	
rust (03) - 17 yds	
metallic copper - 24 yds	
cutting line	

Bottom Side (12 x 15 threads)
(stitch 10)

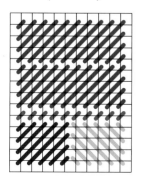

Top Side (11 x 6 threads)
(stitch 10)

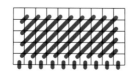

Bargello Coaster Set

A four-way bargello pattern makes a stunning design for our coaster set. With its casual elegance, you'll want to use it every time you entertain.

oaster Size: 4¹/₈"w x 4¹/₈"h each

older Size: 4⁷/₈"w x 1³/₄"h x 4⁷/₈"d

pplies: Worsted weight yarn (refer to color key), two
)¹/₂" x 13¹/₂" sheets of 7 mesh plastic canvas, #16 tapestry
edle, cork or felt (optional), and craft glue (optional).

tches Used: Gobelin Stitch, Overcast Stitch, and Tent Stitch.

structions: *Use lavender for all joining and to cover unworked
ges.* Follow charts to cut and stitch Coaster Set pieces. Join Top
des along short edges. Join Top to Top Sides. Join Bottom Sides
ong short edges. Join Bottom to Bottom Sides. If backing for
asters is desired, cut cork or felt slightly smaller than Coaster.
ue to back of Coaster.

esign by Joan E. Ray.

COLOR (NL)		COLOR (NL)	
white (41) - 15 yds		burgundy (03) - 25 yds	
pink (07) - 15 yds		lavender (05) - 40 yds	

Coaster (28 x 28 threads)   (stitch 4)

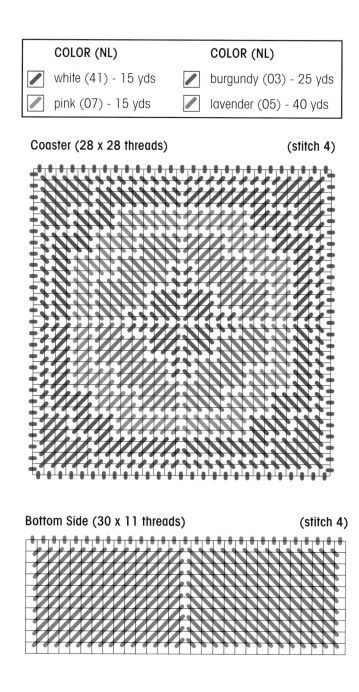

op Side (32 x 6 threads)   (stitch 4)

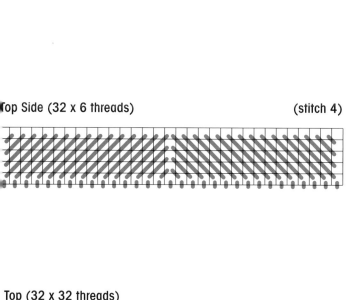

Bottom Side (30 x 11 threads)   (stitch 4)

Top (32 x 32 threads)

Bottom (30 x 30 threads)   (stitch 4)

Kitty Coaster

Our cute cat coasters will be welcome at snacktime—or anytime! This "purr-fect" set even features a handy basket for storing the friendly felines.

COLOR (NL)	
✎	lt tan (16) - 15 yds
✎	black (00) - 6 yds
✎	cat color -12 yds

Skill Level: Beginner

Coaster Size: 4½"w x 3¼"h each

Holder Size: 4⅜"w x 1¼"h x 1½"d

Supplies: Worsted weight yarn (refer to color key), one 10½" x 13½" sheet of 7 mesh plastic canvas, #16 tapestry needle, cork or felt (optional), and craft glue (optional).

Stitches Used: Backstitch, Cross Stitch, Overcast Stitch, and Tent Stitch.

Instructions: Follow charts to cut and stitch Coaster set pieces. Matching ✖'s, use lt tan to join Side to Bottom. If backing is desired, cut cork or felt slight smaller than Coaster. Glue to back of Coaster.

Design by Sue Penrod.

Cat Coaster (27 x 31 threads)

Bottom (27 x 9 threads)

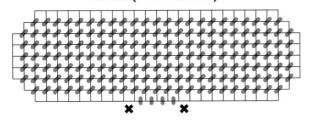

Side (62 x 8 threads)

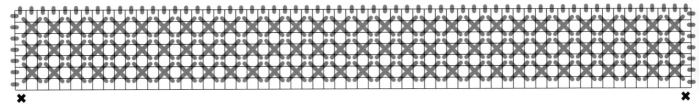

Fruit Basket Favorites

ur fancy fruit coasters look fresh-picked when displayed in their pretty storage basket. Place one of the sweet accents nder a glass of your favorite beverage as you enjoy the goodness of summer. They also make great magnets when itched on 14 count perforated plastic with 6 strands of embroidery floss.

ll Level: Beginner

prox. Coaster Size: 4¹/₂"w x 4¹/₂"h each

lder Size: 4³/₄"w x 7¹/₂"h x 2¹/₄"d

pplies: Worsted weight yarn (refer to color key), three ⁾¹/₂" x 13¹/₂" sheets of 7 mesh plastic canvas, #16 tapestry edle, 24" of ³/₈"w green grosgrain ribbon, cork or felt (optional), d craft glue (optional).

tches Used: Backstitch, Cross Stitch, Gobelin Stitch, Lazy Daisy tch, Overcast Stitch, and Tent Stitch.

Instructions: *Use tan for all joining.* Follow charts to cut and stitch Coaster Set pieces. For Bottom, cut a piece of plastic canvas 15 x 33 threads. Bottom is not worked. Matching ✖'s and ♥'s, join Sides to Front and Back. Join Bottom to Front, Back, and Sides. Matching ★'s, join Handle to Front and Back. If backing is desired, cut cork or felt slightly smaller than Coaster. Glue to back of Coaster.

Designs by Kathleen J. Fischer.

Continued on page 15.

COLOR (NL)	COLOR (NL)	COLOR (NL)
▨ white (41)	▨ dk pink (62)	▨ yellow green (61)
▨ yellow (20)	▨ red (02)	▨ dk yellow green (23)
▨ dk yellow (57)	▨ purple (45)	▨ tan (43)
▨ orange (11)	▨ dk purple (46)	▨ brown (13)
▨ dk orange (12)	▨ green (28)	◯ dk orange Lazy Daisy (12)
▨ pink (55)	▨ dk green (27)	◯ black Lazy Daisy (00)

Apple (28 x 33 threads)

Lemon (33 x 25 threads)

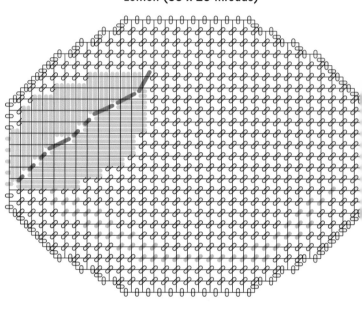

Orange (31 x 31 threads)

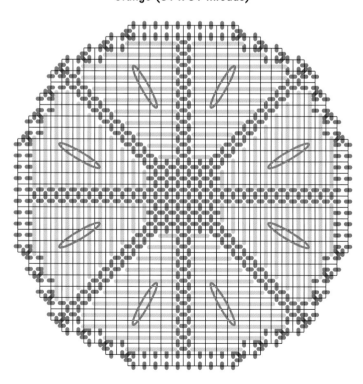

Grapes (32 x 34 threads)

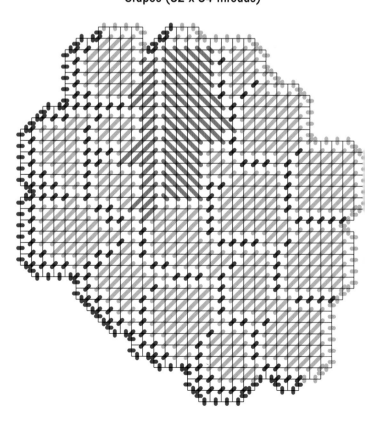

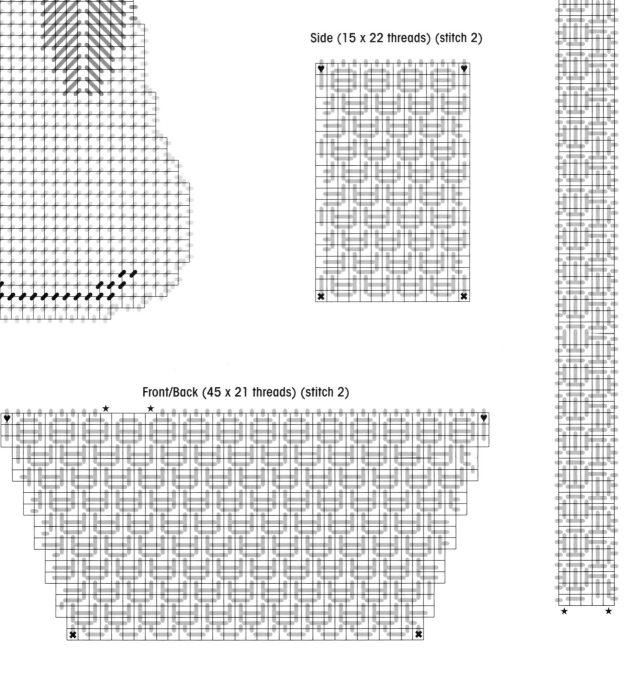

Watermelon (31 x 31 threads)

Handle
(6 x 71 threads)

Pear (26 x 39 threads)

Side (15 x 22 threads) (stitch 2)

Front/Back (45 x 21 threads) (stitch 2)

Garden Fresh

"Sow" this garden patch of coasters and reap a bumper-crop of compliments! The farm-fresh patterns will add homegrown appeal to your kitchen table.

COLOR		COLOR	
⬛	ecru	⬛	green
⬛	gold	⬛	dk green
⬛	lt orange	⬛	lt brown
⬛	orange	⬛	*lt brown
⬛	dk orange	⬛	brown
⬛	lt purple	⬛	dk brown
⬛	purple	⬛	*dk brown
⬛	blue		*Use 2 plies of yarn
⬛	lt green		

Skill Level: Beginner

Size: 4¹/₄"w x 4¹/₄"h each

Supplies: Worsted weight yarn (refer to color key), one 10¹/₂" x 13¹/₂" sheet of 7 mesh plastic canvas, #16 tapestry needle, cork or felt (optional), and craft glue (optional).

Stitches Used: Backstitch, Overcast Stitch, and Tent Stitch.

Instructions: Follow charts to cut and stitch Coasters, completing backgrounds as indicated on chart. If backing for Coaster is desired, cut cork or felt slightly smaller than Coaster. Glue to back of Coaster.

Designs by Kathleen Hurley.

Beet Coaster (28 x 28 threads)

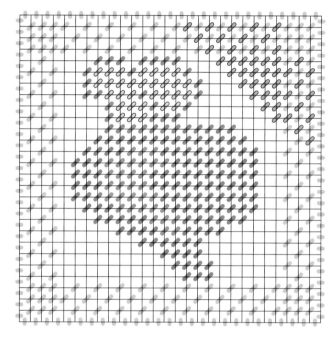

Green Pepper Coaster (28 x 28 threads)

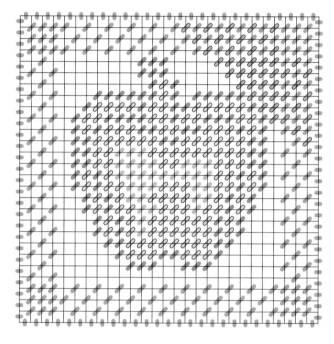

Mushroom Coaster (28 x 28 threads)

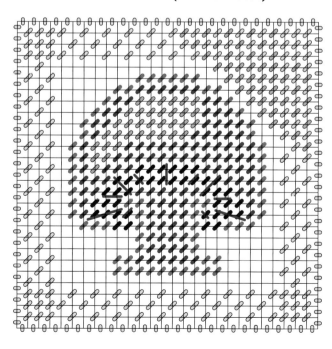

Pumpkin Coaster (28 x 28 threads)

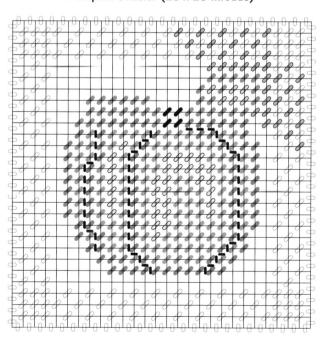

Romantic Rose

Enjoy the timeless romance of flowers with a cabbage rose coaster. This never-fading blossom offers pretty protection for your dressing table or other fine furniture.

COLOR	COLOR
white	lt green
vy lt pink	green
lt pink	dk green
pink	*dk green
*dk pink	*purple French Knot
blue	*Use 2 plies of yarn

Skill Level: Beginner

Size: 4¹/₈"w x 4"h

Supplies: Worsted weight yarn (refer to color key), one 10¹/₂" x 13¹/₂" sheet of 7 mesh plastic canvas, #16 tapestry needle, cork or felt (optional), and craft glue (optional).

Stitches Used: Backstitch, French Knot, Overcast Stitch, and Tent Stitch.

Instructions: Follow chart to cut and stitch Coaster. If backing is desired, cut cork or felt slightly smaller than Coaster. Glue cork or felt to back of Coaster.

Coaster (28 x 27 threads)

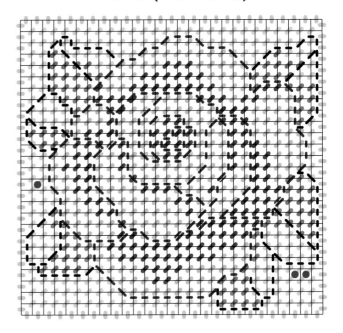

Home Sweet Home

This homey coaster captures the charm of Colonial Williamsburg. Stitch a set and create your own tabletop village or present them to a new neighbor as a thoughtful housewarming gift.

COLOR (NL)	
/	ecru (39)
/	red (01)
/	blue (35)
/	dk blue (48)
/	dk grey (38)

ll Level: Beginner

e: 4¼"w x 5"h

pplies: Worsted weight yarn (refer to color key), one 10½" x 13½" eet of 7 mesh plastic canvas, #16 tapestry needle, cork or felt otional), and craft glue (optional).

rches Used: Cross Stitch, Gobelin Stitch, Overcast Stitch, and Tent ch.

tructions: Follow chart to cut and stitch Coaster. If backing is sired, cut cork or felt slightly smaller than Coaster. Glue cork or felt ack.

Coaster (28 x 33 threads)

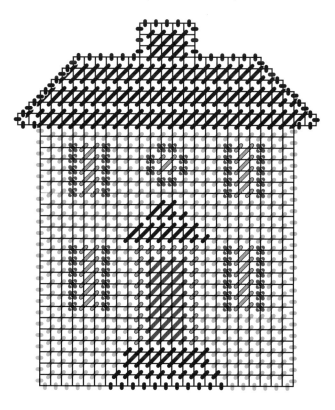

Quilt-Block Coasters

Crafted in the spirit of a traditional American art form, our handsome coasters will add old-fashioned flair to your living room or den. You can stitch all six for a homespun variety or create a set using your favorite quilt block patter

Skill Level: Beginner

Size: 4"w x 4"h each

Supplies: Worsted weight yarn (refer to color key), one 10¹/₂" x 13¹/₂" sheet of 7 mesh plastic canvas, #16 tapestry needle, cork or felt (optional), and craft glue (optional).

Stitches Used: Diagonal Mosaic Stitch, Gobelin Stitch, Overcast Stitch, Scotch Stitch, and Tent Stitch.

Instructions: Follow chart to cut and stitch desired Coaster. If backing is desired, cut cork or felt slightly smaller than Coaster; glue to wrong side of Coaster.

Designs by James R. Green.

COLOR (NL)	
⟋	ecru (39)
⟋	blue (35)
⟋	dk blue (48)

Coaster #1 (26 x 26 threads)

Coaster #2 (26 x 26 threads)

Coaster #3 (26 x 26 threads)

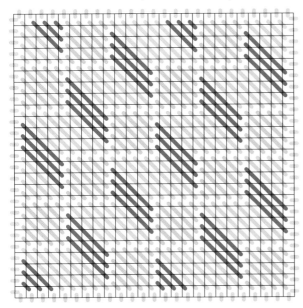

Coaster #4 (26 x 26 threads)

Coaster #5 (26 x 26 threads)

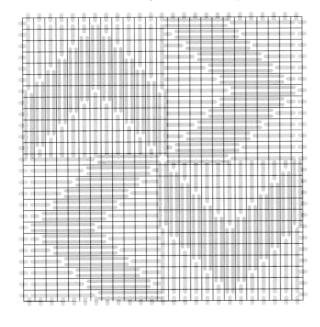

Coaster #6 (26 x 26 threads)

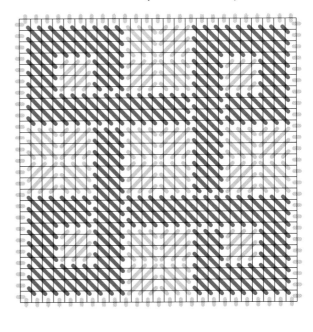

Hobby Coasters

It's a breeze to delight the hobby enthusiasts on your gift list with a set of quick-to-stitch coasters. There are designs perfect for a seamstress, an artist, a card player, and a pianist!

Level: Beginner

...rox. Size: 4¼"w x 4¼"h each

...plies: Worsted weight yarn (refer to color key), one 10½" x 13½" sheet of 7 mesh ...stic canvas, #16 tapestry needle, cork or felt (optional), and craft glue (optional).

...ches Used: Backstitch, Gobelin Stitch, Overcast Stitch, and Tent Stitch.

...ructions: Follow chart to cut and stitch desired Coaster, completing background as ...icated on chart. If backing is desired, cut cork or felt slightly smaller than Coaster. ...e cork of felt to back of Coaster.

...wing Thread design by Teresa E. Barnett.
...ist Palette design by Cheryl Krepps.
...dge design by James R. Green.
...no design by Michele Sartain.

COLOR (NL)		COLOR (NL)	
white (41)		blue (32)	
yellow (57)		green (28)	
orange (58)		tan (16)	
red (02)		grey (38)	
purple (45)		black (00)	

Sewing Thread (31 x 31 threads)

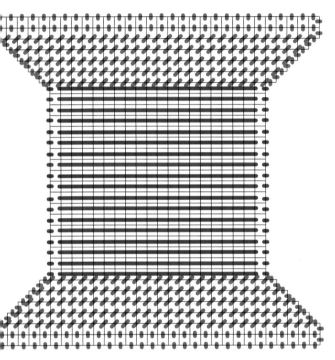

Artist Palette (30 x 30 threads)

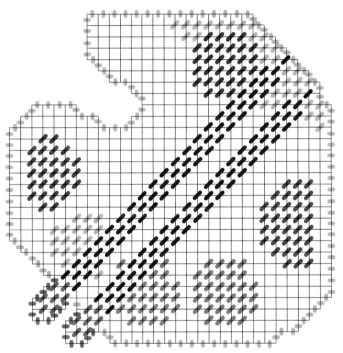

Bridge (27 x 27 threads)

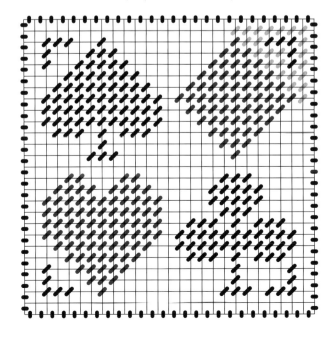

Piano (27 x 30 threads)

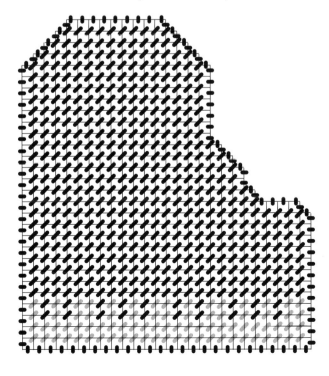

24

Tacking. To tack pieces, run your needle under the backs of some stitches on one stitched piece to secure the yarn. Then run your needle through the canvas or under the stitches on the piece to be tacked in place. The idea is to securely attach your pieces without your tacking stitches showing.

Uneven Edges. Sometimes you'll have to join a diagonal edge to a straight edge. The holes of the two pieces will not line up exactly. Just keep the pieces even and stitch through holes as many times as necessary to completely cover the canvas.

STITCH DIAGRAMS

> **Unless otherwise indicated, bring threaded needle up at 1 and all odd numbers and down at 2 and all even numbers.**

Backstitch
This stitch is worked over completed stitches to outline or define **(Fig. 2)**. It is sometimes worked over more than one thread.

Fig. 2

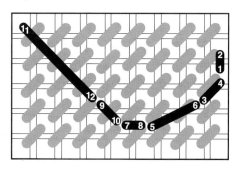

Cross Stitch
This stitch is composed of two stitches **(Fig. 3)**. The top stitch of each cross must always be made in the same direction.

Fig. 3

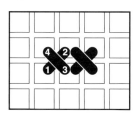

Diagonal Mosaic Stitch
A variation of the mosaic stitch, this stitch is worked in diagonal rows as shown in **Fig. 4**.

Fig. 4

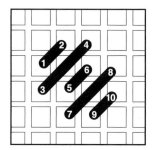

French Knot
Work French knots over completed stitches. Come up at 1. Wrap yarn once around the needle. Insert the needle at 2 and pull it through the canvas, holding the yarn until it must be released **(Fig. 5)**.

Fig. 5

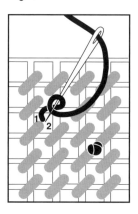

Fringe Stitch
Fold a length of yarn in half. Thread needle with loose ends of yarn. Bring needle up at 1, leaving a 1" loop on the back of the canvas. Bring needle around the edge of canvas and through loop **(Fig. 6)**. Pull to tighten loop **(Fig. 7)**. A dot of glue on back of fringe will help keep stitch in place.

Fig. 6

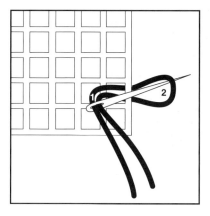

Fig. 7

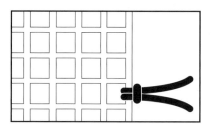